Wild and Free

Mick Manning and Brita Granström

W
FRANKLIN WATTS
LONDON•SYDNEY

Tigers are protected – but they could still become extinct unless poachers are stopped.

Who could live in a world without tigers?

Not Gita! Gita lives in India. She has only seen tigers in books, but she needs to know they are out there – living with their cubs in the dark forests. Wild and free.

Who could live in a world without sharks?

Not Lee-Anne!
Lee-Anne lives in the USA and she thinks sharks are cool – sharp fins slicing through the oceans.
Wild and free.

White sharks are becoming very rare. They are usually harmless to humans but sometimes mistake swimmers for their favourite food – seals.

Who could live
in a world without wildcats?

Not Angus! Angus lives in Britain and
dreams of seeing a wildcat someday –
leaping through the windy heather.
Wild and free.

Wildcats are meeting tame cats and breeding with them - this means that soon there may be very few true wildcats left.

7

Who could live in a world without whales?

Not Atsku! Atsku lives in Japan. She
wants to go on a whale-spotting holiday
to see them – such huge animals,
breaking the waves.
Wild and free.

8

Whale numbers are growing now, but whales still need protection.

Who could live in a world without bears?

Not Anita! Anita lives in Spain and once she
saw a sad brown bear at a circus. She hopes
bears will stay in the mountains – far away from
hunters and circuses.
Wild and free.

10

There are a few bears left in some European countries, they are extinct in many others.

Who could live in a world without gorillas?

Not Essi! Essi lives in Africa and her ambition
is to see a silverback gorilla – swinging a
toddler in his arms.
Wild and free.

Who could live in a world without rhinoceroses?

Not Mo! Mo lives in Africa and he hopes to see a rhino one day. A rhino with a huge horn on her nose and a small calf by her side – gallumphing across the plains.
Wild and free.

Rhinos are killed because some people think their horns can be made into magic powder.
There are not many rhinos left now...

Who could live in a world without cougars?

Not Jake! Jake lives in Canada.
Sometimes he imagines
he really is a cougar –
a golden cat padding
through the Rocky
Mountains.
Wild and free.

Cougars or mountain lions are shot because they sometimes kill cattle and sheep.

Who could live in a world without koalas?

Not Luke! Luke lives in Australia and goes to sleep dreaming about koalas – shinning up the trees carrying their babies 'piggy-back'. Wild and free.

The eucalyptus trees koalas need for food are disappearing. Other dangers include bush fires and dogs on the hunt.

19

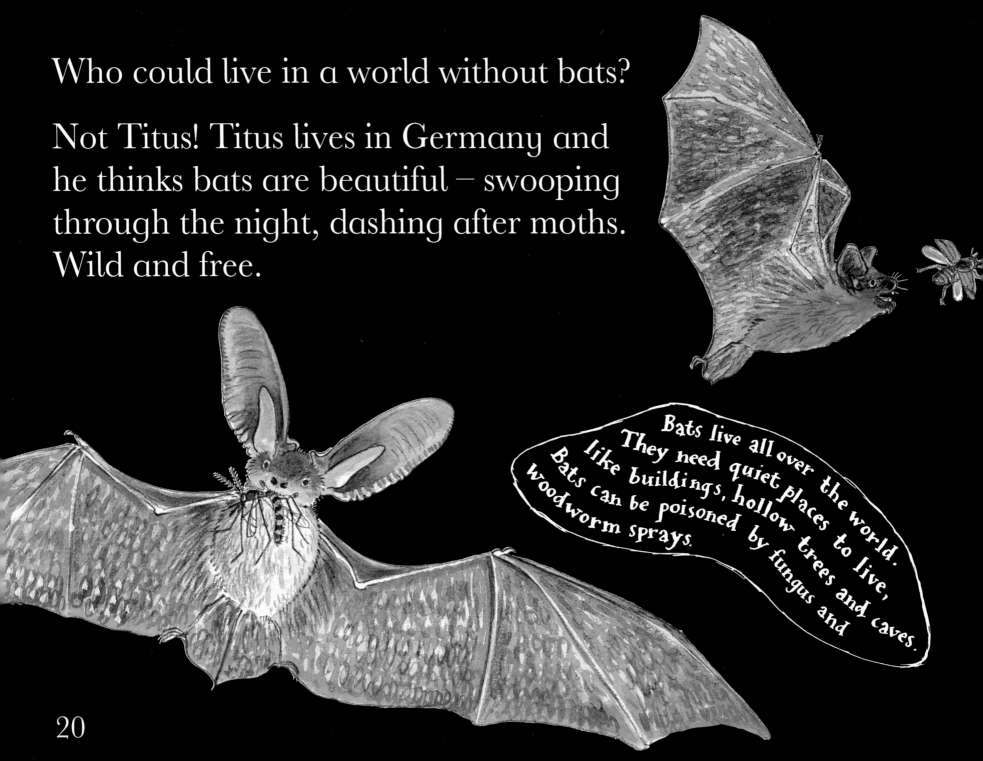

Who could live in a world without bats?

Not Titus! Titus lives in Germany and he thinks bats are beautiful – swooping through the night, dashing after moths. Wild and free.

Bats live all over the world. They need quiet places to live, like buildings, hollow trees and caves. Bats can be poisoned by fungus and woodworm sprays.

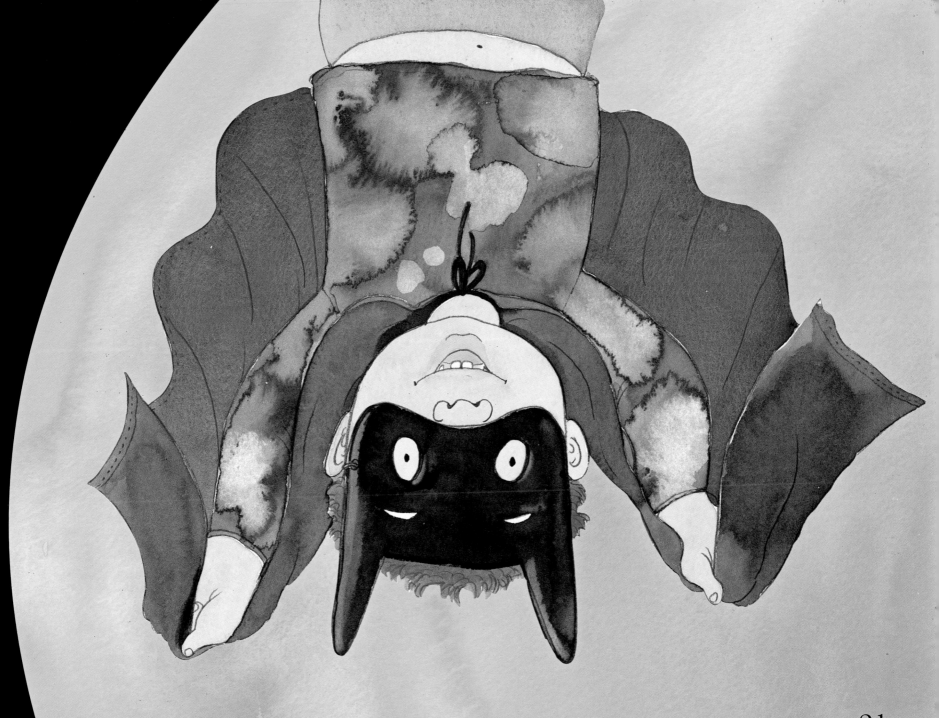

21

Who could live in a world without wolverines?

Not Anna!
Anna lives in Scandinavia
and she would love to see
a clumsy wolverine
one winter's day –
thumping
through secret,
snowy places.
Wild and free.

23

我愛熊貓

Who could live in a world without pandas?

Not Chen!
Chen lives in China and he loves pandas. He wishes they could be safe and happy — eating bamboo, sitting in their forests.
Wild and free.

Who could live in a world without jaguars?

Not Maria! Maria lives in South America. She hopes the jaguars and the rainforests will soon be protected forever – the jaguar prowling in the rainforest. Wild and free.

Jaguars need the rainforest to live and hunt in. But some of the rainforest is being chopped down to make furniture and burned away to make room for cattle.

27

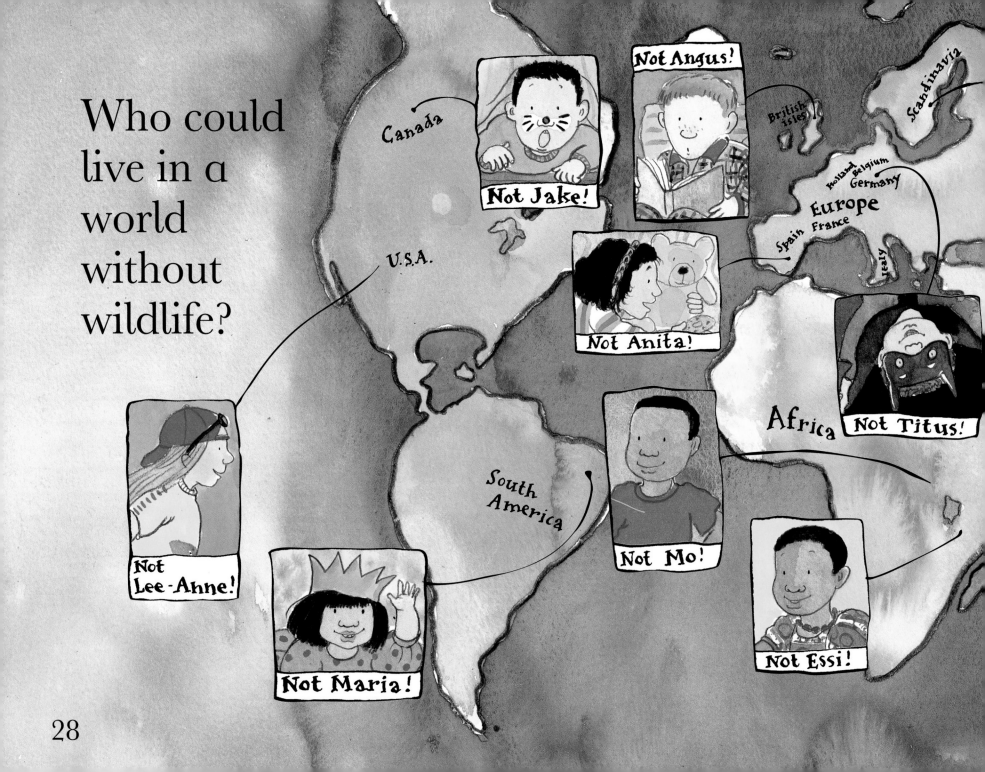

Who could live in a world without wildlife?

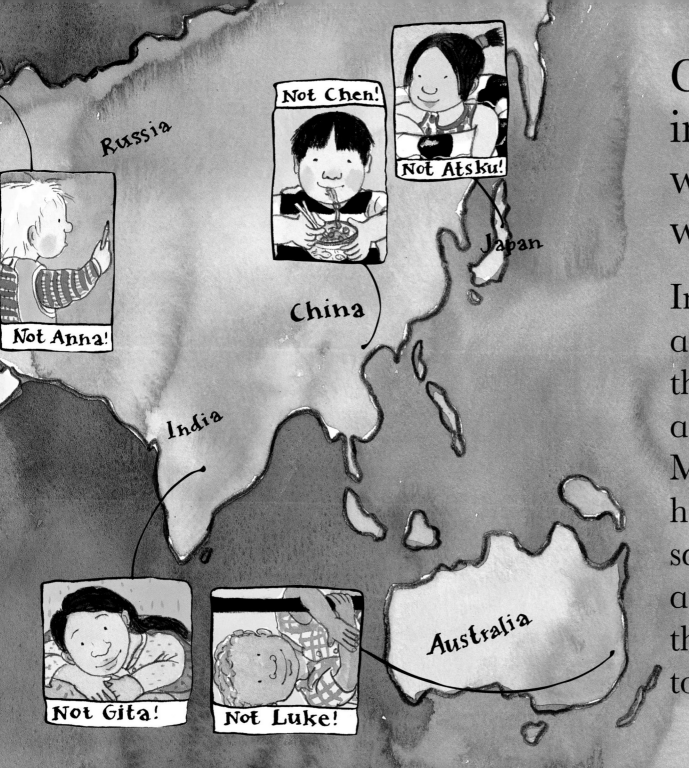

Could you live in a world without wildlife?

In this book there are just a few of the animals that are in danger. Many animals have already been saved, but there are still thousands that need our help to survive!

29

Helpful words

Breeding is when an animal has babies (see page 7).

Extinct means that an animal is gone for ever (see pages 2, 11).

Fungus A mushroom is a sort of fungus. Some fungus grows on wood and stone in buildings causing damage. Sometimes it is sprayed with poisons to kill it (see page 20).

Habitat is the place where an animal or plant needs to live.

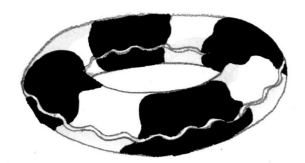

Poachers are people who kill animals that are protected by laws. By selling a tiger skin and its bones or a rhino's horn, hunters can get more money than they would earn in a whole year! This tempts some hunters to break the law and become wildlife poachers. Rhino horns and tiger bones are bought to make expensive powders that some people believe to be magic medicine (see page 13).

Population is a word to describe the number of animals in a place. For example, you could say the 'squirrel population' in a park, or the 'wolf population' of the USA.

Protection helps rare animals to survive. Protecting animals means providing quiet places for them to live called nature reserves; passing special laws to stop them being hurt or disturbed by hunters, and making sure they have enough to eat and somewhere safe to raise their babies. To protect an animal population we have also to protect its food and habitat (see pages 2, 9, 13, 24, 26).

Rainforests are huge areas of forest bigger than some European countries. Sometimes they are called 'the earth's lungs' because they give off clouds of the oxygen we all need to breathe (see page 27).

Rare an animal is rare when there there are not many left in a place, or a country or even the whole world (see pages 5, 24).

Species is a word to describe types of animals – like whales or dogs.

Wilderness is large areas of wild country all over the world where people don't live and there are few roads (see page 23).

Wolves are surviving in some parts of the world but in other places they have been wiped out. Farmers shoot them for killing sheep and cattle, but wolves really like to hunt deer and rabbits (see back cover and title page).

For Max Ivar Manning

If you would like to know more about animals in danger and how to
help you can contact:
World Wide Fund for Nature International (WWF)
Avenue du Mont Blanc
1196 Gland
Switzerland

First published in 1998
by Franklin Watts,
96 Leonard St.,
London EC2A 4RH.

Franklin Watts Australia
14 Mars Rd
Lane Cove
NSW 2066

This edition 1999

Text and illustrations © 1998 Mick Manning and Brita Granström
Series editor: Paula Borton
Art director: Robert Walster
Printed in Singapore
A CIP catalogue record is available from the British Library.
Dewey Classification 574.5
ISBN 0 7496 2990 8 (cased); ISBN 0 7496 3459 6 (paperback)